The Arctic Diaries
Melissa Davies

ARACHNE PRESS

First published in UK 2023 by Arachne Press Limited
100 Grierson Road, London, SE23 1NX
www.arachnepress.com
© Melissa Davies 2023

ISBNs
Print: 978-1-913665-74-6

eBook: 978-1-913665-75-3

The moral rights of the author have been asserted.

All rights reserved. This book is sold subject to the condition that it shall not, by way of trade or otherwise, be lent, resold, hired out or otherwise circulated without the publisher's prior written consent in any form or binding or cover other than that in which it is published and without similar condition including this condition being imposed on the subsequent purchaser.

Except for short passages for review purposes no part of this publication may be reproduced, stored in a retrieval system or transmitted in any form or by any means, electronic, mechanical, photocopying, recording or otherwise, without prior written permission of Arachne Press.

Cover © Natasha Emily Lynch 2023

Printed on woodfree paper by TJ Books, Padstow, England.

Thanks to Muireann Grealy for her proofreading.

The publication of this book is supported using public funding by the National Lottery through Arts Council England.

MIX
Paper from responsible sources
FSC
www.fsc.org FSC® C013056

Bird Wife, Halibut, Seaweed, The Look Out Men and *Værøy* previously published in *Time & Tide* Arachne Press 2019

For Matthew

Thank you for your unwavering support of my writing and for agreeing to 'run a creative retreat' with me in the Arctic. May you never have to defrost another desalination system.

The Arctic Diaries

Contents

Introducing Fleinvær	8
Guide to *Norsk*	9
Part One	11
18th November – We Arrive	
Fleinvær is Made up of Three Hundred and Sixty Five Islands	13
Into the Archipelago	14
Bird Wife	16
Sær Orm	17
(marram grass)	18
An Island is the Summit of a Mountain	19
Værøy	20
Island Birth	22
The Lookout Men	23
Treasures From the First Boat	24
A Disturbance Recounted Years Later	26
The Fisherman Remembers a Boy Disappeared	29
Equinox	30
Skrei Season on Røst	31
Stranger	32
When they Closed the School	33
The Fisherman Remembers the Boy Reappeared	34
Vær, or Island Weather	36
Part Two	37
4th January – We Listen	
Vanishing Act	38
Made into an Island	40

Fiskebruk	41
Halibut	42
Immersion	44
Coffee	45
Seaweed	46
(Collecting)	47
i. *The Artist Collects Fish Bones*	48
ii. *The Fisherman Collects Feathers*	49
iii. *The Musician Collects Guests*	50
iiii. *The Fisherman's Wife Collects Books*	51
Guardians	52
Preparing to Leave the Island	53
Said the Father to His Wife, the Mother	54
Part Three	57
16th April – We Leave	
Poppel	58
A trawlerman recalls	59
Flomålet	60
They Call Him the Salmon King of Norway	61
Langholmen	62
(Out of the Archipelago)	63

Introducing Fleinvær

Fleinvær is a real place – an archipelago off the Arctic coast of Norway. As well as being one of only a handful of inhabited islands in Fleinvær, Sørvær is home to *Fordypingsrommet*, where I spent the winter of 2018-19. The fisherman and his wife, musician and artist are all fictionalised characters based on the people who welcomed us into their homes many times during those dark months. While all the stories, myths and events referenced here are theirs, on more than one occasion I have embellished them with details pulled from research or my own imagination. All I ask is that you don't read this as a work of historical fact but then, as the title suggests, neither is it entirely a work of fiction. *The Arctic Diaries* blends the two using my experience of Fleinvær and the picture I have pieced together from the stories its residents chose to share with me.

With a complete lack of young people, the folk and environmental knowledge of Fleinvær will be lost in a matter of years. By writing *The Arctic Diaries*, I hope to give some of their stories permanence and a life of their own. The current struggle to keep the archipelago's fragile community from destruction at the hand of Norway's 'Salmon King' only makes it even more urgent to share their experience. However, I will remind you that every word written here comes from the pen of an outsider.

January 2022

Guide to *Norsk*

Øy/Øya	Island/The Island
Sundet	Sound or strait, as in water separating islands or connecting two larger bodies of water.
Skrei	A type of Atlantic cod which migrates south from the Barents Sea and is fished around the Lofoten islands from January to April. The name is shared with the word *skrei* meaning 'to migrate'.
Tørrfisk	Stockfish, air dried cod famously exported from the Lofoten and Vesterålen areas of Norway.
Hjell	Wooden racks used for drying *tørrfisk*. In winter coastal areas of Northern Norway are stacked with row upon row of racks, each heavy with *skrei* tied at the tail in pairs. The flesh cures in the cold, but not freezing, air of these islands.
Fiskebruk	A building, containing a refrigerated area, where the fisherman of Fleinvær store their catch before transportation to the mainland. The few residents of the archipelago also have their post boxes there.
Tang	Seaweed
Sær Orm	An unidentified sea monster, similar to the selkie or Scottish kelpie. A direct translation is 'sea worm' but often sightings mention horse heads and details such as a mane or fins.
Finbiff	A traditional Saami dish using diced reindeer meat and juniper berries.

Poppel   The sharp point of waves created when tide and wind are moving in opposite directions.

Flomålet   The black line, usually bare rock, between snow and sea left by the receding tide. *Flo* = high tide *mål* = measure or space.

Flein   Bare, bald or barren.

Vær   Traditionally means weather but can also be used to refer to a small village or community dependent on the sea.

Part One
18th November – We Arrive

Fleinvær is Made up of Three Hundred and Sixty Five Islands

which I count off with calendar cross tongue flicks on my front teeth
to pronounce their suffix for straits. They soften it with a
flourish of ink
mimic sea flowing smooth around headlands of canvas—
inanimate and complete as headstones, slowly slowly
erased islets in their hundreds. Without purpose names survive
only in the tongue flick and fluting of wind through open lips.

Into the Archipelago

Follow me down Nautøyleia with an easy paddle
at our backs Rødøya

Helløya the sister
burnt low and rust sheathed

barely land   the afterthought of dusk
                  best seen from Løksøya lookout island

Store and Litle Skakkholmen
                      these spits that count for days

as boldly as the yellowing hump of Ansøya.

*

See islands spliced by rights to graze
thrown against ownership as it washes westward

blue eye of a cormorant
mistaken for their missing child

                      becomes the story once shared
                      on a low tide crossing

watch it seep into juniper roots and bog
as we cross Ansøyasundet by the flock route

coming now to Fleinvær's heart.

*

Ours is Sørvær

smell diesel fumes from its single boat
a fisherman who sent his son to Tromsø
                                          with photographs

you decide if the weight here is sodden moss
        lives   or damp south breath
from the mountains beyond

keeping these bodies
where they have always been.

Bird Wife

Otter belly brushes snow
filling wood gaps
with warm otter smell.
Daylight slips through glass weights
caught in plaster,
breath makes the orb opaque
as she cries
                on the porch.

Otter in the eider house knows
language left with the fisherman.
Leaking from his tongue
silver strings shivered into buckets
guts from a spring catch.
Otter nesting in eider feathers,
bird wife wailing into storm wind.

Sær Orm

Her tablecloth is *sær orm* skin
scavenged where the sea
washes rocks in spring tide
wool felted by fists of waves
woven with hairline veins that map
every muscle twist of the monster.

Eye—cup—mouth—a knife,
slipping stories under coffee stains
lost fish scales and sea kale

    whispers of deeper water

a pig of navy leather
dissolves to a reeking slime
                    on land.

Priests collecting stories come to collect.
She folds the skin along crease lines
in her imagination.

      where the sand meets earth she bends
wrenches a fist of marram grass to feel the blades slip between
the life
lines of her palm

the other hand gathers spines of sea thrift for colour

An Island is the Summit of a Mountain

They say the fisherman has never known mountains
yet he has spent his entire life on this island
watching from the summit.

Here they speak ascents in dialect,
survive titan's rage with knowledge
of the valley bottom beneath.

Distance is only
space taken
by water.

Værøy

It's the weight of the mountain
forcing them to stay on the edge
with their soft flesh and felt clothes
houses built from trees
for the illusion of being solid.
A man chips tiles from the skin of cliffs

but it's the weight of the mountain
that shelters him from wind
from needles of salt
from sliding away with the bitter
tangles of kelp that crawl back
towards the water at high tide.

Stuck in the throat of the mountain
light belches east every spring
on the warm breath of the sea.
Wool here is woven close and heavy
to crack on a shin
snatch against an unshaven jaw

scoop winter rains or flakes of *skrei*,
herring and the round stones
of Mollbakken. Peripheral treasures.
Yolk of an eagle's egg slithers
down butts of gneiss while the shell
quivers in the salt grass glade.

The man lays down the chisel to see
Moskenøya calve his horizon
into opal halves. He imagines climbing.
Talons curling over the rim of the fin,
calluses slip on smooth worn
stone beneath. He is the eagle.

Here on the peak he sees
the lost egg, the flash of sun
from a pair of fish carcasses swaying.
Here too the weight of the mountain
always draws their soft flesh and scales
to the bone edge.

Island Birth

In a feather storm she bleeds
while they watch from the window.

Umbilical cord lashed around reed fine bones
smearing mother over moss;

a barely life traced in hot sweet ribbons.
There's no cruelty in taking eyes

that have never seen
                              Raven tells Crow
but all they hear is the screech

scrape beak edge of birds feeding
on the just-born lamb.

The Lookout Men

Her father's father was a lookout man on Løksøya,
the lookout island, watching the sea his whole life
with his back to his wife (who came from the agricultural
district of Helgeland but lost a brother to the sea
alongside sixty-eight Filipinos, three Swedes and a Brit).

Her father was a lookout man on Løksøya,
riding the low tide west he'd flicker out of sight
for breathless minutes while he bound the boat
scrambled up goat tracks to watch the horizon.
She felt juniper needling through wool

while she waited for his seawarped lean on the hill.
She knew his back by heart. Better than her mother
or her mother's mother, who didn't bother to look.
'That little patch of bare earth was my doing,'
they would say when she was discovered,

'I know the prickle of juniper on kneecaps,
I can hold my breath for the time one man
takes to reach that lookout peak and
I have seen more than they have
without once crossing that fjord.'

Treasures From the First Boat

They ran circumferences
before knowing
what circumference meant.

Knowing only folk in cabins
at the centre
of their fifty-pace world.

They ran with wind and gulls
straight into water
seeing no border, just more space.

They ran to meet the first boat
hoping to trade
feathers for treasures.

They ran to meet more boats
after hearing about castles
built from fish spines

trees spread over entire countries
horses with branches
growing out their skulls and children

filling streets with music
when the king passed through.
Children who never learned to swim.

They ran coins down cracks
in rocks known by heart
but already irrelevant.

They ran lengths of their world
as it continued to grow,
every step feeling more on the edge.

A Disturbance Recounted Years Later

for Antoon C. Oudemans

The fisherman pulled an oarfish
from his net, its bladder ballooned
a rubbery bubble of saliva.
Blood turned to jelly overnight.

He scooped the stinking mass
back into water where it hovered
as globules, thickening wind
into white-capped waves.

*

Sea monsters appeared
in calm weather, calm water.
Holding their heads aloft, a mane
or maybe seaweed on a seal.

Gliding on a plane of cloudy slack
otter tail, whale gait.
One woman found a skin
tangled with kelp and tar.

*

Sea monster took a leg.
Fisherman's uncle, one-footed captain
from Mervær caught a sunfish
in his lobster pot.

Hear the plastic stump—
round, boot, round, boot.
Snow tracks, sand on deck
he spilled the bucket of shark-oil paint.

*

Blood turned to fire overnight.
Scorched moonlight and pools
of paint beading
at the foot of the boat house.

They gathered in a ring
around strange from the deep.
A mystery to men who have seen
every sickness of the sea.

*

In grey stillness they sailed,
steel creak on oiled wood
of crowds on a turning tide.
Scale stars and eyeballs twinkled

his wife ran a finger down the fin.
Round. Boot. Round. Boot.
Blade jangled against pail in the climb
whispering shingle as the first hull thumped.

*

They gathered in a bigger ring
around strange from the deep
holding their heads aloft
blood turned to salt on the dirt.

Sunfish cut from the lobster pot
heaved scrunch shingling
slice of flesh and warmth spilled
stinking of southern water.

*

A missing catch, a leg and a story.
Dawn tracks of saliva on sand
still stinking of southern water
and the current that carried it north.

The Fisherman Remembers a Boy Disappeared

After one month it's assumed he drowned. We are used to this but without a body, a closing, his family cannot return to the sea. Instead they punish it. Driftwood limbs are thrown back to deeper water, nets torn to regurgitate their silver cascades and crab pots are left to rot on their ropes. Every life they take from the sea they return to the tide as death until water takes on blood tang in spray on their lips and rust replaces salt in their elbows. After two months food parcels are left by islanders who see starving brothers stealing eider eggs but I share the yolks which we eat hidden behind a derelict boat house, wiping our glossy fingers on its boards. The brothers carefully pick flecks of paint from the creases of their palms before returning to their mother. After three months their father dies. We stand on the kai while two boys heave his naked body over moss towards us, I said they should row him out to open water. Instead they go back to their house and we stay to watch grit settle over the dead father's eyes.

Equinox

Imprisoned by a freak tide quick spring hope drowned in brown waves that shake their window on the orders of a barrel moon. Splinters tap glass. Water pries apart months like planks on the quay but the fisherman waits for his ally to accept her distance once more. His confidence is contained in painted frames of stillness. She will withdraw this veil of kelp and earth that divides his seasons.

Skrei Season on Røst

Keen cod-tongue cutters in white fingered rows
trimming between catches and classes.

They came with the *skrei*. Countless vessels
colliding with shoals from the Barents Sea,

children poured across bog filling timber space
with ocean chaos.

He spoke of history—tales their parents recited
on black afternoons while they waited for the sun.

Some years they waited for *skrei*. More often wind
pinned boats to bays while children screamed

about shipwrecks and sea worms. Winter hair wild with salt
obscured features, family names. Permanence.

In April the teacher watched shoals dwindle,
bay water slacken, quays and desks clear once again.

Stranger

No wind in his hair,
they told parents.

                The children
gave him a cormorant feather,
a jaw bone
found on the beach
still with its teeth.

They couldn't identify it
neither could he.

                The teacher
who took the 6.07 ferry
while children ate oatmeal
and stolen eider eggs
off tired kitchen tables.

When They Closed the School

she stole canvas wall maps rolled into brass cylinders,
dust still stuck in a ghost star over the archipelago.

The Fisherman Remembers the Boy Reappeared

Four months earlier
a mother's fist
scarlet against snow
pounded grief
and something like regret
only darker
more tangled
in blame.

Her nails tore
rock black moss
threads of water
tracing anguished veins,
we strained to join her
in that place
but I was only
stood beside a rock.

Now those scarlet fists tear
her returned son's clothes.
Deaf to our questions
the boy insists again,
'I've been living in there.'
He points to the boulder
smothered by moss,
'With the lady in the rock.'

When she laughs
    the mother
I remember a *skrei*
caught with a hook
piercing its eye
viscous shudders
tore its resistance
to spatters of hot blood.

Four months
writhing in the net
of her own skin
left it taut and cold
    the boy
brittle as glass
on her shoulder
looking for another.

Vær, **or Island Weather**

Think of tarpaulin
slapping wind thick with bursts of sea spray,
ropes jumping waves like hounds restrained.

Think of juniper
knee high and gnarled into fists,
barrier from ocean end to Sørværsundet.

Think of slate,
tissue paper squares on gales whipped
across this scatter of barely land.

Think of words
at the centre of this whirling world.
Think of the words they've created

through need to explain
rain that tears wood planks while gifting
driftwood and the knowing of every single mile

like a breath from your own lungs—
visible, real. But impossible to capture.
To be lost without loss.

Part Two
4th January – We Listen

Vanishing Act

after David Morley

How can you know what it is like to lose
your magic? When surviving here was an act
set up by fishermen with no view beyond sea.
Their rope frays between your fingers
until a single thread holds your whole animal
reason to continue. You row your knuckles raw
at midnight, daylight or anytime your children alight
on the quay their great-grandfather built,
simply to keep them coming back, and listening.
How can you know when it's time to accept
they were never listening? They can't believe
in sea monsters or boys hidden in stones—
only dry skins swinging from cod-racks in wind
where once they gathered dried flesh for food.
These stories of sunfish are pulled from hats
of salt-dumb old men while their fingers
finger rings from crab pots and your children disappear.
How can you know what you will feel
when it's over? Grief as the last spectator leaves,
relief that your son will never learn to make one *skrei*
feed four children when only half the shoal reappear.
Your eagle's eyrie is a pile of sticks
every needle bone must be collected before they bend,
while you can still see whole animal bodies.

How can you know who will stay on this island
without you? The bird ate her children before returning
to the mainland. You should eat your children
if it would make your magic stronger,
bring the sheen back to your velvet sea
and shoals dazzling like sequins under limelight.
But when dry wind blows across your open palm
all you can taste is bone dust.

Made into an Island
                                              from the Latin *Insulatus*

They talk about isolated incidents. Are you an isolated
incident entirely unconnected to those islands
on your horizon? I defend your history which is more of a
geography of shoals following storms
following tides following lunar cycles. Remembered in
a language I don't understand. They talk about isolated
incidents but I hear outdated, inefficient, difficult to
standardise or monetise.
Let's talk about archipelagos.

                Insular communities—unfairly described
while your livelihood arrives from blue grey distances carrying
flotsam and creatures, stories from
environments you try to understand. Washed up sunfish
you'd have missed with your back to the sea,
these shelves of books would be landscapes of the landscape
reflected with liquid eyes. They talk about isolation
in the alphabet of landlock.

                Island winter is measured in *skrei*
yet you haven't met a quota since Lofoten quays clattered
with crates and gasoline dialect. They talk about behavioral
isolation; perfected over seven decades through two sons and
a failed salmon farm. Talk to me
not for healing, I can't bring the curlews back but I can keep
your memories from seeping between the roots
of pines you planted as a child. When your island is a forest
                      this page
                      will connect us.

Fiskebruk

He's explaining the *fiskebruk*
but all I can think about is the fisherman's
filleting knife slipping under my epidermis
flicking individual bones out in experienced
                                    exquisite rhythm.

Halibut

                        Fifty-six halibut tails.
Grotesque imitations of butterflies
tough as the nails pinning them down, ashy from winter rain or
spring frost. Some have split too far, begun to peel apart.
Mermaids
cursed with legs, stumps of scales fringed by ochre flakes of meat
nodding on an easterly breeze.
The man who owns the hammer
        only comes here in summer.

A successful halibut catch
is always preceded by sex.
These petrified fish tails
are notches on a headboard
                                    only
      it's the same woman every time.

One fin overlaps others, taking four nails to restrain cartilage
centimetres thick, petrified fingers contracted to form shadows
angular, sinister but still fragile
as skin off my palm.
                                  I'm certain
this one preceded the conception of a child.

In folklore the halibut is wise
a giver of sound advice

I'm told by the fisherman's wife
who birthed four sons on this island

yet no tails hang from her walls.

Immersion

Hours later she can feel
a bracelet of droplets
freezing
on her wrist.

Ache clings to joints,
fish scales to her fingers.

Pearls of ice
crunch
between teeth
and steel.

Delicately she picks bones,
spits grit from the blade.

Tomorrow, she swears
again,
she'll send him
emptying crab pots.

She could take a boat to the city
just to feel concrete under foot.

Cold pattern sting on her skin
knows
she probably
won't go.

Coffee

Grounds slip between our teeth
from coffee stored in Thermos jugs.
They're not bitter. Yet the taste always
summons shipwrecks and sea birds,
        equinox tides that submerge.

Tonight, following a full moon,
waves knock at the timber house window.
His story twists into dialect.
                      Spits me out.
Words for the summit under a maelstrom,

for currents tearing islands apart
or shapes of water over a shoal
pour like breath between us.
The fisherman's voice ebbs, pauses
        returns to language that falls heavy

but familiar in my cupped hands.
When another candle goes out
his story ends. I gather it quickly
before the smoke feather dissipates
        and light shows only dregs in our mugs.

Seaweed

So black against the snow
I can taste the summer *tang*.
Roll
       tiny bubbles
with the new shape
of my tongue.

Saliva rushes
to meet the salt
of their language.

*Every creature on Sørvær is a collector.
On the island I also find myself compelled to collect
and discover that our hoards have a similar composition.*

i   ***The Artist Collects Fish Bones***

Guests and their stories
pass through his studio on the sea
with the printing press,
promise of *Finbiff* (reindeer stew)
if they fascinate him.

The artist stores paintbrushes
in jaw bones and bird skulls.
He stores his memories
in those people who listen
in those people who leave.

ii   The Fisherman Collects Feathers

Yesterday they burnt a boat damaged by storms,
fibreglass smoke billowing past seagull screams
    signal smoke billowing across the strait.
He stood beside Magne's bridge to smell dark grey waste,
hear the boat's story trickle through shingle
between their foreign words and music felt in his gut.

Tomorrow they'll catch a ferry back to the city
leaving sandpipers picking crumbs of plastic from fire pits.
An eider will try to nest in remnant heat while tar
sticks her chicks to feathers he waits all year to collect,
'The king of Norway sleeps in a duvet of Fleinvær down!'
But their engine devours the fisherman's voice like diesel.

iii   ***The Musician Collects Guests***

until the ghost of his brother
has been stretched to the size
of a room beneath his ribs
and no one will ever stop talking.
Through a horde's beer roar
he continues to rehearse
scales on steps in winter
scales on steps in wind
in rain until fingertips replace
what he cannot forget and the clarinet
slips into heartspace or cracks
against Kebony panels where it's thrown
forcing him back to his party.

iv   The Fisherman's Wife Collects Books

1.

I send one. Picture it pressed between wood and paper,
flattened back to new beside a volume on tree identification,
Saami folk tradition or cooking with *tørrfisk*. The cover is thin,
cheap print that feels like slightly more than another page.
It won't travel well. Waves of damp will swell each leaf
while it waits out weather in her post box over the sound.

2.

Once she showed me a photograph;
brass clock on white board wall
beside a postcard of Ithaca. Around the image a sentence and space,
whiter than anything on this island
whiter than anything she had known,
it felt more vast than the sea we could hear through timber walls.
Clean. Intentional. An Arctic of imagination—
not this place of moss and juniper, amber skies
melting into pools of kelp and always those coils of blue rope.
He came two winters ago, she told me, with his camera.
Speaking German.
Seeking forgotten places or forgotten people, she didn't know.

3.

I hope she takes my book off the shelf
and tells of the couple who stayed for a winter.

Guardians

A *sær orm* skin hangs
from branches of pine trees
planted by the fisherman
as a child.

Through tangled needles
translucent leather shivers;
frost sealed and secretive
guardian of *hjell*.

Watcher of *skrei*—
row on row of bodies drying
in a Barents wind sway
from A-frame racks.

The fisherman's wife collects
brittle fillets in a basket,
takes the monster's skin
for her table.

*

A bowl of ivory flesh
weighs her skin cloth flat
while ancient elbows
pin it down.

A display of pine cones
drips needles so fine
they lodge in creases
and the silvering beards

and the wool cuffs of her guests
carry them along with talk
of what they saw at sea.
One saw a moonfish beached.

Another, stroking the skin,
swears of a lady sailing
in crab shells between islands.
A seal left its skin on a rock.

*

But without children their tales
catch in the fisherman's pines
or scatter back to sea
on that Barents breeze.

Meanwhile flakes of *skrei*
fall from the bowl
onto a fish skin cloth
which is only a cloth, after all.

Said the Father to His Wife, the Mother

We're waiting for the curlew
to return to our island,
straining for the call that completes us.
You watch the spring sky
though I tell you it's sea
not wind on a journey that far;

and we agree that it's far
we've come waiting for a curlew?
I fail to feel time now sea
is our clock and our calendar an island
but you insist that our sky
is timekeeper who protects us.

So you look up to protect us
while I still hope from afar
it's not down to your sky
to show us our curlew,
or admit while we are on an island
our lifeline will come from the sea.

Can you help me to see
why an ocean stands between us
when we're sharing an island?
Why loss has forced us far
apart, unless we're talking about curlews
or you're staring at that sky

and I'm telling you, save sky
hopes, while we pick through sea
gifts for a sandpiper or curlew
feather discarded when they left us
to snow storms for pine trees far
taller than any on this island.

Our isolated land we call island.
Where we married and cried into skies
full of life, wondering how it could feel so far
from where we'd been before. Even sea
appeared dead to us
until we watched the whirling curlew

and knew our son wasn't far from his island.
His curlew's eye remains in our sky,
his voice in the sea that surrounds us.

Preparing to Leave the Island

You pile rocks against the light hours
while I swing buckets of salt over timber
to preserve these weeks

Heaps form around our ankles and I'm sick
every morning when I see them

You heave another rock and tell me it's our future
not the taste of salt water nor *tuttbær* jam

sticking like dialect in our mouths
those will fade you say   Already
my salt is seeping back into the sea

Part Three
16th April – We Leave

Poppel

Salt water droplets flick off razor crests
                forcing attention to the horizon
                            from sea soaked fingers
      but the trawler is several hundred metres
                from his boat   still

fresh waves spill pink below the gutting plank
                where he watches a competitor
                        cleave shoals out city harbour
the fisherman's knees bend to agitated sea
                lost scales flash in bristle

He counts eight neon figures as they gather to haul
                      breaking the grey length of day
                beside his feet crates groan with each lift each
        drop
        eventually the old man leans on the helm and drifts
                      to avoid their lines.

A trawlerman recalls...

Before, I hauled timber from coastal forest south of the circle.
Went home with sweet pine on my coat, hands stiff with sawdust
before blood and oil dried there. Salt weather slowed work
sucked water from saplings, made the forest poor so I followed
the wind west before I was pushed.

> Now my lips crack when I smile.
> But I still count in tonnes.

Flomålet

falling water sings in black as bare rock emerges
blank phrases sustained until lunar flip reverses
her repeated melody

        fisherman records a trickle over limestone
        tidy notes of an otter's claw
        catching between moss knots
        marram calling in snow wind
        an old rope's sigh as it sheds blue strands
        one by one by one
        he collects the scream of sea eagles
        passing overhead when once
        they stopped on the island
        crack underfoot distracts his microphone
        becomes the opening note
        for this latest composition

from a distance black between pause of snow
and teeming roiling frothy symphony of life sea
snatching opportunity

for a living the fisherman goes further
to currents that still gather shoals
for music he stays where he knows
feels juniper berries purpling his back
that should be feeding a chorus of birds
beneath his fingers limestone murmurs
he hums with an engine drone
knows this must be preserved
not a sky of reeling wing beats
nor echoes of their abandoned future
but every wave break pebble roll between
roaring life and the silence that follows

always water sees easy gains on emptiness
she sends up a wave of salinity
and the black phrase fades from sight

They Call Him the Salmon King of Norway

The salmon king blew a hole in the hill

as his island sea filled
fishermen came to watch their reflections rise in the void

sea can't be trapped they told him
rolling lumps of limestone into respectful mounds
around the wound

                yet they could see that in fact it had.

Langholmen

Juniper clutches a seagull feather
yearning towards open water,
                              years of tides
      lift its weathered claws
only to fall

        six hours later.

Trees are patient though,
the spring moon is waxing.
Soon fjords will swell beyond their fill
and juniper can soar on silver-tipped wings
                              once more.

We're squinting north to Valan now

where whirlpools swallow sounds
and names have been forgotten

                        or swept
into dense channels   straits

curdled with flotsam of the half-remembered
                    lilting on the tide

towards Havsundet
the fjord that opens to sea.

Acknowledgments

For Odd and Nina, whose stories continue to fuel my desire to write. Thank you also to Håvard, without whom I'd have never set foot on Fleinvær; to my parents for raising me to create not just survive; to the New North West Poets whose feedback and support has shaped more than one of these poems; to the Society of Authors for giving a mother time to see her project through. Lastly, Fern, I hope this has been worth the separation and that in understanding you find inspiration of your own.